T0153004

Dwellers in the House
of the Lord

Also by Wesley McNair

Dwellers in the House of the Lord

of the Lord

A Poem

Wesley McNair

David R. Godine, Publisher
BOSTON

Published in 2020 by
DAVID R. GODINE, PUBLISHER
15 Court Square, Suite 320
Boston, Massachusetts 02108
www.godine.com

Copyright 2020 © by Wesley McNair

All Rights Reserved.
No part of this book may be used or reproduced in any manner
whatsoever without written permission from the publisher, except in
the case of brief quotations embodied in critical articles and reviews.
For more information, please write to the address above.

LIBRARY OF CONGRESS CATALOGING-IN-PUBLICATION DATA

Names: McNair, Wesley, author.
Title: Dwellers in the house of the Lord : a poem / Wesley McNair.
Description: Boston : David R. Godine, Publisher, 2020. |
Summary: "In this book-length narrative poem, award-winning
poet Wesley McNair takes us to rural Virginia, where his
younger sister Aimee is adrift in a difficult marriage to Mike,
an off-the-grid gun shop owner. As Aimee grapples with self-
doubt and searches for solace in a vacuous megachurch, Mike's
misunderstandings are magnified by the self-first ideology and
fear-of-others philosophy swirling around him. McNair casts this
intimate family struggle against Trump's noisy public race to the
White House"-- Provided by publisher.

Identifiers: LCCN 2019051065 | ISBN 9781567926637 (paperback)
Subjects: LCGFT: Poetry.
Classification: LCC PC3563.C388 D84 2020 | DDC 811/.54--dc23
LC record available at https://lccn.loc.gov/2019051065

FIRST PRINTING, 2020
Printed in the United States

For my sister.

Part I

1 ·

Inside the box she sent is bubble wrap
folded over and over around
a thick envelope, awkwardly folded,
and deeper down, wrapped
in Christmas paper with my name
on top in a blur of letters
handwritten over and over,
my younger sister Aimee's late gift,
sealed in an old plastic bag
like a secret she wants only me
to know: a silver charm bracelet,
which in the winter light of my kitchen,
dangles a palace, a running horse,
a heart with a key, and a clock.

Once, after returning from a long visit
with our mother, Aimee, married
with two daughters, hid under her bed,
keeping herself a secret. Mike searched
and called for hours before she called back
at last and he found her, discovering also
his unshakable, lifelong anger at the woman
my sister had tried to put out of her mind.

But Mike was her replacement
for my mother.

A mind has so much to keep track of:
which secrets to share,
which to guard from others,
and now, who and where anyone
is anymore. In Aimee's letter—
creased and re-creased from
her underlining and afterthoughts
in the margins—she asks me to mail
her Christmas cards for my children,
having forgotten their addresses
and their names. *They can't hear
my chattering*, she writes,
*but can read of several things
I wanted to write <u>inside</u> <u>the</u> <u>card</u> <u>itself</u>.*

The Lord loves you, she remembers
on the back, where a single heart
floats in a blank sky.

2 ·

In the famous family photograph,
Aimee sits on the couch beside Mike
in his Navy uniform, holding his hand
and looking up at him with the defenseless
wonder she wore all though girlhood.
Eight years old, she has just asked him
to marry her. Nobody would have guessed
he would come back later to do it,
or that he would take her to live with him
north of a Navy base in rural Virginia,
his smiling, clean-shaven face now
overgrown by an unkempt, anti-social beard.

Outside the back window
of Aimee's second house
from the time they moved in,
the high, dangling chains
and gambrel stick
of a deer-slaughtering station.
In the front, open all day,
Mike's gun shop. "Obama
is going to make me rich,"
he says one night, chuckling
on the phone before handing it

to Aimee, "but I'm already
out of bullets. Everybody
down here's out of bullets."

Behind his chain-link fence, two dogs,
penned for life without names
so they won't be spoiled for hunting.

3 ·

One fall day in Claremont, New Hampshire,
my stepfather, who came with his family
from Quebec, Canada, took me and my brothers
to visit a Polish family in a triple-decker
apartment without enough windows to throw
off the gloom. The father produced two glasses
for drink, and at the edges of his storytelling
and gesticulation, Mike, a quiet boy my older
brother's age, emerged beside his mother,
who dragged one leg, because of a stroke
she suffered as a young woman, I later learned,
and still later, from Mike, that she never

touched him except with a switch,
yelling at him in Polish for breaking her rules,
and each week made him bring her, as if
it were his fault, the half-empty bottles of vodka
his father had hidden in the hall closet, or behind
the toilet, or under the front seat of the car.

It took only ten years for the new K-Mart Lawn
and Garden Center at the mall off route 89 to destroy
the nursery business my stepfather and my mother
had built. Afterward he lost the anger he learned
from growing up as an immigrant, and the defensive
tilt of his chin that said I'm better than you
and I'm no good at the same time. Opening himself
at last to the defeat he feared from the start,
he went back to his job on the night shift
at the same shop where his father worked
until he died. No one could reach him. Even when
my mother, grown desperate, blamed him for quitting,
he was silent, wearing the dazed look of a man
who'd awakened in the dreamlife of a stranger.

"Listen to her brag about getting food stamps,"
Mike shouts to Aimee, who's in the kitchen
while he watches a black woman
with two children in Virginia Beach on TV.
"She can't even talk right," he says.

In the presidential campaign of 2016,
two stories: on one side, the uplifting
American Story of the Immigrant,
on the other, a darker story
derived from the failures of the first,
both of them our stories.

4 ·

For years the two of them drifted
toward each other, Mike dulled
by alcohol on submarines, Aimee
looking for a home. At age 21,
she ended up in a bathtub

in the projects of Claremont
with a French-Canadian husband
who stooped over her, starting up
a hair dryer and threatening
to toss it into the water with her.

Meanwhile, at 35, Mike spent
an entire leave and all his money
on a bar stool in Naples, Italy,
barely recalling his wife and stepchildren
back in the States. Closer now

in their drift, Mike, retired from the Navy,
wakes up in Abner, Virginia, as a Jehovah's
Witness with half his life gone to drink,
saved by Alcoholics Anonymous
and an angry God devoted to fire

and retribution. Divorced, like him,
Aimee is back home with her father,
who named her, now an old man gone silent,
and her pitiless, faultfinding mother,
more convinced than ever that the only

life left for her is her reconstructed
daughter's life. Driving to another town,
Aimee walks up four stairways of a tall
building and jumps off the roof, breaking
her ankle, her leg, and two vertebrae.

Waking in the trash of an alley, she feels
the excruciating pain of her body,
which is also the pain of still being alive.

This is the moment my fragile sister thinks of,
lying in the dark for hours under her bed
after returning to Mike from her mother's house,
with no place else on earth to hide.

5 ·

But before that lying in the dark,
she must lie in the zero
of a white room at the hospital,

bandaged and lost to herself.
And when at last she opens

her eyes, she finds Mike sitting
beside her, and sitting there
again the next day, just as he sat
when she was a child wishing
he would take her far away,

and after she reaches out to hold
his hand, and they go on talking
over weeks in their low, intimate way,
sometimes kissing, it becomes clear
that he will marry her and actually

take her, though the far away place
turns out to be Abner, where,
she learns in time, the anger lives,
first Mike's upset with a barking dog
next door, which he threatens to shoot

with such determination, Aimee
convinces him to start again
in another house, quieter,

she tells him, farther away, but there
she finds herself alone with his rage.

"Why," I ask my declining sister
on the phone after unwinding
and unwrapping the gift she mailed,
"did you send me the charm bracelet
I gave to you when you were a girl
with a dream of horses and going off
to the palace, like Cinderella?"

"Because I kept on losing it," she says.

6 ·

At age thirteen, after my mother, two brothers
and I moved into my stepfather's tar-papered
garage-house, I began to paint the creche scene
on its temporary picture window, guided
by the illustration on my mother's old church
program. Each afternoon as the school bus

slowed to a stop by our driveway to drop off
my two brothers and me, I saw again
the growing forms and colors of robes and canes
and donkey's ears and cross beams of a manger
transform our sad home in the snow,
no longer a place of anger, but of anticipation.
Everyone felt it, because as I painted the mantle
of Mary and the face of the Christ child
she gazed down upon, my mother was newly
pregnant. It was Aimee who lifted us up
all through the winter and into the spring
when she was born, the daughter my mother
had always wanted, and the baby sister
with braids and a smile in the framed
photograph I carried to each college dormitory
and apartment after I left my stepfather's house.

Yet this baby who smiled every time
my brothers and I held her
and spoke to her, cried herself to sleep
night after night, while our mother,
who inherited the fierce look she wore then
from her own mother, refused to hold her
so she wouldn't cry again.

Twenty-five years later, Aimee had Sophia,
named after Mike's mother, then Lena,
giving birth also to a love and hope
that went deeper than the fear she felt
for herself, though now she was afraid
for her girls. Each day as they grew up,
she lifted the invisible wet finger
of her worry, testing for currents
of inclement weather inside her house.
"'Don't bother your father,' is what I say
on the bad days," she tells me on the phone.

"He's never hit anybody," she adds,
to comfort me. "I don't think
he ever would."

In the photo Aimee mailed of her yellow
and orange beech tree in the fall,
I see for the first time the house in Abner
where she started again. Over one
of its two front doors, a sign says GUNS.

7 ·

*This is my favorite tree—it bears leaves all
year round*, Aimee wrote on the back
of the picture she sent, meaning, I understood,
how the beautiful leaves flung high above
the house had nothing to do with the troubles
inside it, like Lena's drawings of birds,
which sometimes made her cry, she told me
later in a phone call, they were so hopeful.
But on the day she called about the church
she and Lena and Sophia had found, Mike now
busy behind the kitchen door in his gun shop,
it was she who was hopeful, the bright tones
of her voice still in my mind. "It wasn't strict
and plain like Michael's church," she said,
"it was made from somebody's home, with a funny
tin hat built onto the front of it, and when
we went inside, it felt mismatched and comfortable
like a home. The worship room, you could see,
used to be two rooms," she said, "and there were
curtains on the windows beside pictures of Jesus
and the heart of Jesus with a key in it, and rows
of mixed-up wooden chairs and different-colored
plastic chairs." But what really struck my sister,
she said, was the woman who started weeping
while the preacher, Pastor Chris, was leading

the hymn about Christ's love, "weeping so loud
she said, "that Pastor Debbie went over and held her
and I started to cry, too, right in front of the kids,
because I saw that the woman without love
was me! And then," she said, "midway through
Pastor Chris's sermon about the loving mansions
in the palace of heaven, this old man stood up
and began shouting things that scared me
at first because they didn't seem to make any sense,
until I finally saw it was his need he meant,
which felt like my own need," she added, whispering it,
"and this warmth started in my chest and traveled
all the way down to my legs like thawing out,
and I stood up with the others and shouted Amen—
I couldn't help it, Wesley—Amen for the man,
and Amen for everybody around me in this church
out in nowhere, which felt like a loving mansion, too!"

Longing was what Aimee learned when she returned,
often by herself, in the months afterward, how
if she shut her eyes as Pastor Chris spoke in his sad
voice about the thirst for Christ's love, she could
almost feel the quenching on her tongue, and how
by standing with her hands out and dreaming

his sermon about the woman who touched the robe
of Jesus, she could sense it on the tips of her fingers,
as if she were no longer bound by time, but awake
in the reborn self He had promised, leaving the one
her mother and Mike had ridiculed far behind.
Sometimes, my sister said, she thought she was a little
like Jesus, each of them hiding a secret awareness
from unbelievers who meant them harm, He
through his parables about new wine skins and fruit
trees, she by telling Mike that God had helped her
find her way, and meaning the women at the local
shelter she visited on grocery days, lingering
afterward beside her favorite field to feed fresh
carrots to the horses. For as years passed,
and my nieces, one by one, left home for college,
Aimee had begun to long for her own life.

8 ·

Being bad, my mother learned
from her own church-going mother
in the Ozarks, was not trying hard enough

to stop being who you were. Being yourself
was what you got slapped for. Yet

when she was seventeen, she, too,
longed to be herself. "I can't wait
to get rid of this family's name,"
my uncle, a boy then, heard her say
in the shack where she lived with her brothers

and sisters. Then she married, had a child,
and headed for New England. Sitting
on a battered suitcase and nursing
my older brother while my father
thumbed rides for the three of them

across the country to a job his cousin
had promised, my mother never guessed
that her longing had just begun.
Four years later, she'd given birth
to three sons and lived in the projects

of Springfield, Vermont, where my father,
moving on, had abandoned her—
she, an immigrant in her own right,

with an accent her Yankee neighbors,
poor like her, strained to understand.

In the late-night quiet when Aimee
began babysitting to pay
for her escape, did she ever think
about the young woman our mother was
before turning into her own mother,

the woman who couldn't wait
to be free, too? Did she remember
her dazed, unfulfilled father at the end
of his life, as I do now, or consider
the longing of the absent fathers

who had left their homes to commute
to city jobs miles away, or the single
mothers doing double shifts at Walmart
or Family Dollar for the children
they so seldom saw? Sitting alone

beside a lamp on the worn sofa
where I imagine her, she doesn't think

of those others at all, only
about the earnings she tallies
in her secret notebook. Yet

on this night in my mind, my little sister,
alone and anonymous in America,
dreams for them all.

Part II

1 ·

I don't know exactly how Mike responds when
he sees Trump for the first time on TV,
but I know Mike. How he might laugh at first
at the ridiculous fake hair, then, just before
clicking to a cop show, get interested
in the way Trump keeps calling the runty
guy from Florida "Little Marco" with a sneer,
and makes them all seem little, especially
the moderators sitting at their desk like teachers
with trick questions: why would Mexico pay
for your border wall to keep Mexicans out,
or what about race relations, their big issue,
while the country goes to hell. In a moment like
watching the bored, disgusted face of Trump
as he turns to take on the moderators, too,
Mike discovers what he's always known:
it's the bullshit rules and the people in charge
who make them up that have been holding him
and the whole damn country back. Now
when he searches on the television for Trump
and finds him wearing a cap over the shock
of orange hair that ignited the anger
he's carried since childhood, he misses it.

But I also know another Mike. Arriving without
family at our camp in Maine for an overnight
after visiting his immigrant relatives in Claremont,
this Mike offers us a jar of his homemade Polish
jam and a larger one of preserved fish. Lacking
his rifle, he is awed by the moose we see foraging
across the pond, and in the twilight that gathers
around our screen porch, he tells us about my sister's
cat, how it can't get enough of her and follows her all
over the house for the chance to lie in her lap.
In this way, having long since submerged the feeling
life that confuses him, Mike confesses his love.

I, too, am confused. I reach out
to the Mike who calls me
Buddy, the Navy name
for friend, and in every secret
phone call, I reach out also
to my sister, bereft and alone.

2 ·

In the summer of 2016, when Donald Trump
appears like a god from clouds of vapor
at his party's convention, Aimee disappears.
Just behind Mike in my mind, as he carries
his hunting rifle into the house and calls
her name, I hear how he senses she's gone
and at the same time denies he senses it, checking
the empty rooms one by one: the kitchen, where
he's sometimes found her under the clock,
staring out the window as if she's forgotten
her hands in the dishwater; the living room
with its still rocker where he's seen her whispering
words he cannot hear to her cat; and finally
the bedroom, where again he says her name,
more to himself, not daring to kneel and lift
the bedspread, as he did long ago, and discover
this time a dark vacancy, like the one that now
opens inside him as he spots the note on her pillow.
In the silence that begins while he lays down
his gun and finds my sister's silent, handwritten
name beneath her reasons for leaving him,
the accusing voice of his mother, which he's spent
a lifetime pushing away, also begins.

One time Michael left the kitchen door open
to the gun shop, Aimee told me,
and a customer was mocking Hillary Clinton
as the ugliest grandmother he'd ever seen.
Her daughter was even uglier, another said.
A third explained why Hillary was a bitch.

When Trump says Crooked Hillary
has accused him of disrespecting women,
the men at the rally stand and chant, *Lock her up!*
"Nobody respects women more than me,"
Trump shouts back to them. "Greatest person ever
was my mother," he says. "Believe me, the greatest."

What the solo demonstrator at a different
rally actually wants is his mother's love,
Trump insists, over and over. "Go back
to Mommy," he repeats with an anger

so personal he seems to be battling
with himself. "Little baby, I can't stand
to look at you," he says, then flips
his hand and turns away, as if he

is the one he has put on punishment.
"Get him out! Get him of out my sight!"
The men in front with bright red
Trump caps lift their fists and cheer.

For who would question the toughness
of a man with his chin thrust out?

4 ·

"The illegals are taking our jobs," Trump says
on the campaign trail in Richmond. "They're
taking everything, including our money.
This is not going to happen anymore."
Build the wall, the audience chants, *build the wall!*

My sister Aimee does not understand politics.
All she thinks about as she starts down the road
she's known for twenty years and sees
the Trump signs is Mike erupting at the blacks
on TV, and the hatred in the gun shop,
and the blessed lightness she feels as she sends

it all, sign by sign, into her rearview mirror.
Beside her in my mind, holding an imaginary cat crate
as she drives toward freedom, I feel the lightness
too, though I worry about the desperation
of the stained double-wide and ruined cape
we pass, and the backyard with bedsprings
and refrigerators and a Confederate flag. Not Aimee.
When I glance over at her, she stares straight
ahead, only turning to look at the broad
green field she loves, where one of the horses
seems to run with us, for after her long struggle
she's living the dream she's dreamed for years.
Never mind the closed knitting factory we approach,
then send behind us, and the big box stores
that replaced Main Street, and the high, indifferent
clock of the Bank of America. My sister is lowering
the windows and singing the old, loving hymn
about being lost and found that we once
learned in our mother's church. And I, the worrier,
the man of little faith, I'm singing it, too.

5 ·

But after Aimee leaves Mike all by himself
with his guns, I cannot stop my worry.
And on the evening of the election, when Trump
sweeps the towns of the Abner area and the Polish
and French neighborhoods of Claremont,
New Hampshire, going on to become President
of the United States, she seems more distant
and fragile than ever. "Please be careful, Baby Sister,"
I tell her on the phone. "Anything can happen."
Yet Aimee wants to talk about all the new people
in the church, her home away from home,
"so many, Pastor Chris preaches three times
on Sundays," she says, "and I teach two
new sessions of Sunday school. I love
being with their children," she says. "But where
do all these people come from? Poor ones,
and needy ones, I can tell by the look in their eyes!"

Awake all night, anxious for Aimee
and for the future of my country, I remember
an old photograph with a deckled edge
and take it from its cubbyhole in my roll-top
desk: me at age fourteen standing outside
the trouble of our home in Claremont
with Aimee as an infant on my shoulders,

the shadow of my older brother on the lawn
as he snaps the picture. In the half-dark
of my study in Maine, far to the north
of her secret apartment, I put the photo
in my printer to scan it for her. Seeing it again
on my computer screen, I can still feel
Aimee's trusting fingers clasp my ears
while I hold her tiny feet in my hands,
as uplifted as she is. *Us against the world,*
I write, then click and send. Up late herself,
she emails back, *Forever, you and me!*

Did Mike find the cat, or did the cat
find him, coming to the woodpile twice,
then peering through the wet dots
that gathered on the kitchen window
while Mike looked back at his green
eyes and wet, flattened ears. "You couldn't
leave him out in the rain," he told Sophia
when she called to check on him.
"And you could guess by looking at him
he was hungry, so I gave him some leftover
cat food," Mike said, not mentioning who
had originally bought the food, or that this

was a tuxedo cat like Aimee's. Sophia
said nothing, just listened to her father
remember each detail of her mother's cat,
now gone, as he told how the two of them
were different, the new cat with a long
white sock and a short white sock
on its back legs, and playful, too,
a word Sophia had never heard him use.
"Dad was just sitting on the couch watching
his cat stretch out on the rug by his feet
calling it my buddy," she told me,
"when he suddenly began to tear up,
which shocked me, because it was the first
time I'd seen him cry. But I got used to it,"
she said. "Back then, he cried all the time."

6 ·

The fourth campus of the megachurch, where
Pastor Chris moved his congregation that winter,
was so big Aimee sometimes felt lost there,
but how else could you bring together so many

people, she said, which was the main point,
after all, not how she felt. And she liked how
the whole staff, from the women who greeted you
at the door to the men who helped the children
and the disabled ones to their seats, never seemed
to stop smiling. "They even have an overflow room,"
she said, "where the organ music is piped in
and the late-comers can have coffee and donuts
while they watch the service on a big TV, while
the other people watch it on the massive TV
in the worship auditorium." Aimee still couldn't
get over seeing Pastor Chris's face blown up
on the screen like that—the same person she knew
from before, yet with a close haircut and a new suit,
plus, looking like he was trying to adjust
to the whole thing himself, the way he kept saying
Amen and Praise God too much, or walking
from the stage to the podium while he was giving
his sermon to check his notes. "Or maybe it was all
me again," she said, "thinking of him as this small
man I saw from the back pacing back and forth
trying to remember his lines, and at the same time
this big authority on the screen saying them—
or what was worse, thinking of myself in the audience
with the camera running, like I was part of a show."

On the Sunday Mike came out of the audience
of the megachurch in his work pants and suspenders
and approached the podium, Pastor Chris
must have been just starting his sermon about how
Christ wants us to win in our lives with the five keys
to material happiness. When I visit the church website
after Aimee tells me about the sermon and click
just above the link with the cross for donations
honoring all credit cards, I watch Pastor Chris
preach the sermon in his slow, sorrowful voice.
But there is no trace on the video of Mike, whose face
on the big church monitor that morning surprised
my sister so much she called from the church
parking lot on her cell phone to tell me about it.
"All of a sudden Michael was up there on the screen
talking to Pastor Chris," she said, "and I could tell
from the red around his eyes he'd been crying, also
that it was all about me, but nobody else seemed
to care, all the ushers wanted to do was to get him
out of the way of the camera shot. Michael
didn't even know what was going on," she said,
"when they turned him around and guided him out
the door. Pastor Chris just went right on preaching,"

she said, now crying a little herself, "so I stood up
and left, too. What kind of a church is that?"

Two days later, when I tell her that Mike
has been erased from the official church video
and she goes online to see, I also show her the link
on the homepage, beside the photograph
of whites, blacks and Latinos standing together
in New Fellowship: a prayer of blessing
and support for President Donald J. Trump.

7 ·

It was clear by then she wouldn't go back
to the megachurch. The bad news,
for me, was she went back to Mike. Again

and again, I imagined her on the long nights
she'd spent babysitting, accompanied
only by her dream of elsewhere,

or rode beside her, just the two of us,
past the Trump signs, as she escaped
from her old life. Where was my little sister?

Who was she? "Aimee, Aimee," I said
to her. "All this time I thought
you wanted your freedom!" But Aimee,

not so little, said, "Freedom isn't about
galloping off into the clouds, Wesley.
It's the chance to make your own choice."

8 ·

On his first days in office, Donald Trump
showed off the words of his executive
orders against Muslims and Mexicans
and healthcare for the cameras
like Vanna White on a game show.

At his winter White House, a golf course
in Florida, he sold face-time

for $200,000. "I can act more presidential,"
he said, "than any president except
the late, great Abraham Lincoln."

Meanwhile, mysteriously, Aimee began to forget.
In the spring, when we went back
to calling each other, she sometimes struggled
with words, and by the fall she was forgetting
whole conversations. Driving to meet Sophia
and take a memory test at the V.A. hospital,
she forgot the way and ended up at twilight
in a parking lot with two off-duty actors
in Williamsburg, outside of the Essence
of America masquerade party, hosted
by Presidents George Washington
and Thomas Jefferson. "For hours we didn't
know where in the world she was," Sophia said,
and I said how glad I was that her mother
had been found at last. But where in the world was I?

In that bleak time of lies and pretending
and grief, I had at least the six words
that Mike, then just back with Aimee, said

when he called me up out of the blue,
awkward, embarrassed, and determined.
I've behaved like a real asshole. In a dark time,
I had this rough, unpredicted truth.

Part III

1 ·

Pick's Disease. Pick's Disease is an
irreversible form of dementia which

can occur in people as young as 20.
Symptoms. Symptoms include reduced

writing and reading skills. Diminished
social skills. Shrinking vocabulary.

Slowed movement. Accelerated
memory loss.

Yet what is my sister, I ask myself
on the winter morning when I receive
the Christmas cards with blank

envelopes for my children,
whom she loves, though she can't
remember their names—what is she

but a soldier against losses?
What has she ever been, putting
her own broken body back together

as a girl, then repairing her broken
heart, over and over, but a master
of trying again, mending,

as her mother, the seamstress,
once mended after my father left,
night after night, to hold herself

and her family together—
Aimee more her mother's daughter
than she ever understood?

2 ·

And so, on New Year's Day 2018, just before
my trip to be with her, I sit in my Maine
kitchen unwrapping her late Christmas present,
the charm bracelet she's sent to me
for my safe-keeping, gradually understanding
the challenge of her gift. For all the silver
charms I unseal and lift out of the plastic
bag where they have been stored—

palace, running horse, key, and clock—
have gone dull, except for the rounded
form of the heart, which shines as I turn it
in the light. I do not know how many times
my sister, caught in lovelessness,
took it between her fingers and thumb
to rub it and make a wish against
the odds, only that the force of her hope
has outlasted the failure of metal and wishes.

3 ·

"Dad's first cat, the one that came to the woodpile,
is Pedro," says my niece Sophia as she drives us
out of the airport. "Lena named him because
the way he sometimes holds his head to one side
with his ears down flat reminded her of a sombrero.
The second cat, which Dad picked out so Pedro
could have a friend, is Baba, his shelter name,
a big old tabby cat. The other two love Baba,"
she says. "Wherever he is, they want to be,
and Dad, too. It's like the damn cat owns the place."

Meanwhile, having left her three-year old son
behind with her husband in Norfolk, she heads
toward the place she means with steadiness
and efficiency, untangling the knots of thruway
that lead us north on 17 to Aimee's sad town
which seems, when we arrive there, motionless
by contrast, its deserted main street now a one-way
to the big box stores at the outskirts, its old brick
knitting factory now rows of vacant windows.
Then, by some turn I haven't followed,
we're twisting through the snowy, hilly roads
of Sophia's girlhood, with trucks in the driveways
we pass and old cars marooned in the yards,
until she swings in behind Mike's pickup
and we're suddenly in her parents' yard.
"Like I mentioned," Sophia says, gesturing toward
the clutter on the porch, "things have slipped
a little since you came a few years back, outside
the house and inside, what with Mom and all."
Then I see Aimee, standing by herself
in a cap and overcoat under the high, leaf-filled
branches of her favorite tree, a study
in winter and faithfulness, waiting, like me,
after all these months of her struggle, to be held.

It was this holding and being held
after her waiting, this looking into her eyes
to find the sister I had always known,
that began to restore me. Walking with her
behind Mike as he carried my suitcase
through that house of forgetting,
past her dusty summer shoes in the hall,
and the living room chairs with yesterday's
sweater on top of the day before's shirt,
and the forgotten Christmas wrapping
and stack of mail on the kitchen table,
I thought about the sorrow of what my sister
had lost and went on losing, but most of all,
about the small miracle of her constancy.

That night after Lena arrived from her work week
at the craft brewery in Newport News, and my nieces
and I sat up to talk, I also thought about Mike,
the husband Aimee chose twice, how even
with the stress of her illness, his face had softened,
and how quick, behind his ragged beard, he was
to smile. Sophia thought one reason was he got rid
of the gun shop to take care of her mother.

"He's always had a soft side, anyway," she says.
Lena nods. "But more now. He's changed."
A cat person like Sophia, she insists
it's because of the cats. "They gave him,"
she says, "the permission to feel."

Aimee is not the only one who forgets. The clothes
in the living room and the old mail in the kitchen
belong to Mike, too. Checking her pills, then
rechecking them as he puts them beside the lunch
he's prepared for her, he confesses that his forgetter
works much better than his rememberer. Yet
he remembers to bring out his box of Polish
memorabilia, which he wants to show me, he says,
because I'm family—old folk dolls passed down
to him, a silver eagle medallion, a bronze
military medal awarded to his great grandfather
on his mother's side, and then, from an old envelope,
a picture of his great grandfather himself, in uniform,
with the medal around his neck. "That was before
they found out he was a Jew and took him away,"
Mike says, "before his children and their kids
fled Poland for the United States." Then he hands me
a photograph of two I recognize: his mother and him

in their home in Claremont after her stroke.
"Whenever she made blackberry or blueberry jam,
I was the one who picked the berries," he says.
"And when she put up her jam or her beet relish
I thumbed in the rubber seals and turned
the lids down on the jars. I was always her right
hand," he says, pleased with himself, pleased
to remember himself with her. "I was her doer."

I do not recognize Mike's father in his photograph,
he is so young, standing on a lawn with a smile
in an academic robe. "When he went looking for a job,
he was turned away because he was a Polish immigrant
and a Catholic," Mike says. "Poor me! Poor me!"
he chants, mocking the black protesters against social
inequality. "Nobody ever demonstrated for him."

"I get your point, Mike," I tell him, passing
the photo back. "His situation was not so much
different from theirs. But on the other hand,
their situation is not so much different from his."

Looking down at his father, Mike does not hear me.
This man who has confessed to me his failings
of the heart, who owns that he is part Jewish,

who has welcomed lost cats with strange-sounding
names into his home, is so close to understanding,
yet does not understand. But we are talking.

At twilight in Williamsburg, two actors, black men,
walk toward their cars with their costumes
tucked away in backpacks, the same two
who discover my sister Aimee wandering alone
in the parking lot. "Who are you?" they ask her.
"Are you lost?" But Aimee keeps asking them
who they are, as if all three of them are lost.
This is the odd scene still in my mind months
after Sophia has described it, Aimee adrift beyond
safety, and the two men released from their play
as black slaves, now set free in America.

5 ·

Given Mike's early trouble with alcohol, he allows
none in the house, but when he and Aimee go to bed,
and what my nieces and I call the night shift begins,

out comes Sophia's cooler with its contraband:
craft beers Lena has brought from Newport News,
and for the moment, Lena is not the graduate
of an art school trying to pay her bills, and Sophia
is not a computer programmer, and I'm not even
their uncle, because we are all in it together
as returning conspirators. Besides, I now see them
as the granddaughters of a Jewish woman who escaped
with her parents from Polish oppression. "You look
a little like your grandmother," I tell Sophia,
and though it's old news, I can't help mentioning
Lena's dark skin, which everyone in the family links
to her great grandmother on my stepfather's side,
the Native Canadian from Quebec. Lena, surrounded
by cats on the couch, sets her beer down, stands,
and pirouettes. "I am a woman of the world," she says.

6 ·

It's hard to tell what Aimee knows and doesn't
know sometimes, looking at you with her eyes
wide open yet speaking as if from a dream,

here, and not here, as she soon will be when we
remember her. Still she is with us, and like the rest
of us, changing every day. When I give her a hug

after she and Lena and I return from our walk,
and she surprises us by calling me Daddy as if I
were her long dead father, has she lost her memory

of me or found a new connection, suddenly aware
that the love she feels is not limited to a single name
or even to the present, but exists in a time

unknown to us, where it all makes perfect sense?
Perhaps when she sits on the couch beside Mike
looking down too long at the cat she holds lovingly

in her lap, or the face of her grandson on the iPad
Sophia hands her, smiling at him with surprise
and joy, she knows more than we think about how

time goes on forgetting her month by month,
and she only wants to dwell in the moments
that move her most. Taught by experience to live

in the world of in-between waiting for the moments
we wish for to happen, we wouldn't really know
if she's letting herself go a little each day to live simply

by touching and holding—by love, the very thing
which, without our quite knowing, she has called us to
all her life, and why each one of us has come.

7 ·

Far in the back of the shelf above the hallway
coat rack, I spot among the other forgotten
hats the unmistakable red of a Trump cap.
I draw it out and uncrumple its message, a call
to arms against all outsiders. *Make America
Great Again*, it says to the wall, where I return it.

At 35,000 feet, Hillary Clinton is on her way
to a talk show in England to promote
her new book about the 2016 presidential

election. High above other clouds, Donald Trump
flies to a speech at a rally in Florida, one more
performance by the damaged maestro
of nobody loves me enough, so seductive
in his aggrievement that his anger and hatred
and longing become their own.

Here on the ground, Sophia is serving supper:
polenta with chicken and vegetables, made special,
she says, from her grandmother's recipe. "Dad
used to make it," she says. I think of Mike, the doer,
stirring polenta for his disabled mother as I settle
into my chair on this, the last evening of my visit.
"Why don't you do the mumbles?" Mike asks, taking
my hand, and, watching him, Aimee takes the other,
joined by Sophia and Lena, and suddenly they're all
bowing their heads, as if I, a practicing disbeliever,
have something to say. "Dear Lord," I begin
from old habit, closing my eyes, and in that dark
find the prayer that rests on my tongue, for us,
and for the refugees who have come before us
from Poland, and French Canada, and the wilds
of the Ozarks, in the arc of the hope of belonging.

8 ·

Taped to the refrigerator in my sister's house
is a seasonal card that quotes the Bible's account
of Christmas. After supper and one last session
with my nieces on the night shift before I go home,
I find the card there once more in the darkened
kitchen, moved by the lopsided heart Aimee has drawn
beside its words about the wise men offering
their gifts at Christ's manger. There is no mention
of the angel who arrives soon afterward to insist
that Christ must leave, which makes this story,
I see now as I end my own story, incomplete.
For we are all born into exile, saved only by the homes
we dream, and the love that we may find there.

A NOTE ON THE TYPE

This poem was set in Janson. Our text face owes its revival to Chauncey H. Griffith of Merganthaler Linotype, 1937. It's been discovered that this type is originally the work of Nicholas Kis (1650-1702), a Hungarian, who most probably learned his trade from the master Dutch type founder Dirk Hoskens. Janson is held in high regard for being both readable and handsome.

Book Design by Brooke Koven

1970–2020
David R. Godine
❦ Publisher ❦
FIFTY YEARS